52 Thoughts
for
Conscious Living

One inspiring thought each week to lead you
consciously through the year

GeniusMedia
CREATING KNOWLEDGE

2020

52 Thoughts For Conscious Living

One inspiring thought each week to lead you consciously through the year

First Edition: October 2020

ISBN 978-1-908293-51-0

Genius Media 2020

© Sonia Samtani 2000 - 2020

Sonia Samtani has asserted her rights under the Copyright, Designs and Patents act 1988 to be identified as the author of this work.

All rights reserved in all media. This book may not be copied, stored, transmitted or reproduced in any format or medium without specific prior permission from the author. Contact Genius Media for review copies and wholesale orders.

Genius Media
B1502
PO Box 15113
Birmingham
B2 2NJ
United Kingdom

www.geniusmedia.pub

books@geniusmedia.pub

www.allaboutyoucentre.com

www.soniasamtani.com

52 Thoughts for Conscious Living

Spring..8
1. Allow the Dark to Experience the Light......................10
2. Light Over Darkness...12
3. Your Mind is the Gateway to Your Wellness...............14
4. Beliefs vs Desires...16
5. Leave Your Past Behind..18
6. Away From Pain or Towards Pleasure?.....................20
7. Are You a Procrastinator?..22
8. Stop Hijacking the Past..24
9. Busting Loose From Your Defense Mechanisms........26
10. Beyond Duality..28
11. Goal Setting..30
12. Making Your Dreams Grow With You......................32
13. Confused About which Path to Choose?..................34

Summer..36
14. Ready? Set? Go!...38
15. Take Baby Steps...40
16. Stay Focused...42
17. Identify your Most Important Tasks.........................44
18. A Different Type Of Prayer....................................46
19. Everything's Gonna Be OK!...................................48
20. Is it Possible to be 100% Optimistic?......................50
21. What's The Worst-Case Scenario?.........................52
22. The Happiness Formula..54
23. Perfect Imperfections..56

24 Intention is Everything..58
25 Failure vs Rejection..60
26 Do You Control Your Destiny?....................................62

Autumn..**64**
27 Manifestation 101...66
28 More Than a Single Thought Creates Our Reality....68
29 Letting Go of a Fear of Failure....................................70
30 Changing your Standards...72
31 Letting Go of Controlling...74
32 Is There a Logical Reason for Illogical Behavior?.....76
33 Being an Adult..78
34 Healing Your Inner Child...80
35 How to Love You?...82
36 Loving Yourself takes More than a Massage..............84
37 Selfish, Selfless, or Self-Love?......................................86
38 Self-Love on Special Occasions...................................88
39 Transitions...90

Winter..**92**
40 The Magic 30 Minutes of Your Day............................94
41 It's OK!...96
42 What Gets You Triggered?...98
43 When is it OK to Scream, Swear and Punch?..........100
44 Acceptance is All You Need to Be Free....................102
45 Surrender – the Only Way to Go...............................104
46 The Play of Opposites...106
47 Clearing Clutter with Emotional Attachment..........108

48	From Pain to Peace	110
49	Leading By Example	112
50	You Have a Choice	114
51	Pause to Reflect on the Year	116
52	A New Beginning	118

About Sonia 120

Some loving affirmations to begin your journey…

I am exceptional • I am deserving • I am loved • I am safe • I am powerful • I am resilient • I am accepted • I am attractive • I am resourceful • I am peaceful • I am worthy • I am amazing • I am supported • I am complete • I am talented • I am grounded • I am believing • I am aligned • I am empowered • I am connected • I am in-flow • I am deserving • I am charming • I am enough • I am beautiful • I am trusting • I am confident • I am self-expressed • I am mindful • I am outstanding • I am accepting • I am compassionate

An Invitation

Sometimes, in the rush of our everyday existence, we can lose sight of the gift that we have that is our mind, and how powerfully we create our reality through all the interpretations and choices we make on a daily basis. When we use our minds to judge, we can easily lose our connection with those around us and feel disempowered. If we could live with this conscious awareness that we are responsible for our thoughts, it becomes much easier to embrace what life has to offer us. We will not operate as victims anymore, and find it easier to accept ourselves, accept others, and accept what comes our way.

This book is intended to give you conscious tools on how to embrace life and keep evolving. You can read it in the seasonal flow as it's presented to you, or open up to any page that inspires you and trust that you are receiving the perfect message for you at that moment.

Each chapter has a thought for the week, explaining a concept and sharing with you an invitation to take action during the course of the week, so that you continue embracing your life in the most rewarding way possible. Some of the concepts are reminders of what is logical, and some are new paradigms of thought that I have tested with myself and my clients and seen beautiful results. I invite you to try on these new concepts like a new outfit; if you like yourself in it and it feels good then keep it on. If for whatever reason you don't think it's "you", feel free to remove it.

The most important thing to do is keep going, to keep turning the pages in your life, to keep enjoying new discoveries, and keep contributing who you are to the world.

Each person's life purpose is unique. You are unique, your life is unique, and you are the only person in this world with your special set of experiences, talents and gifts. Your unique place in this world is expressed in how you fully embrace your essence, and share your gifts with others around you, to make tomorrow brighter, warmer and more empowering for us all.

Consciously yours,

Spring

A time for new beginnings. The first green shoots emerge from the darkness, a time for increasing warmth, for reaching out, for connecting and for exploring. A time for celebrating and appreciating your limitless, wonderful potential.

1 Allow the Dark to Experience the Light

We all know that life is a ride of ups and downs. Some days we're pinching ourselves to see if the beauty around us is real, and some days everything feels like it's falling apart. If you find it easy to accept when things are good, do you also allow yourself to acknowledge without judgment when things seem not-so-great?

Many of us have this unconscious tendency to judge ourselves when we feel sad or frustrated. We tell ourselves that we shouldn't feel anything that isn't 'good' or positive. We feel obliged to put on a brave face, and when someone else says they are feeling down, we say things like "don't feel like that"! Have you ever stopped feeling down because someone has said, "don't feel bad"? The feeling doesn't go away! It actually makes you feel worse because you are adding a layer of judgment to your own experience. For instance, you add a layer of guilt on top of your upset.

Like the passing seasons of the year, or the passing of night and day, your up and down feelings are part of a natural cycle. To embrace and love your whole self, you need to realize that both your comfortable and uncomfortable emotions are valuable. What would it be like to simply observe your feeling with awareness and allow it, knowing it will soon pass over and be another experience?

Invitation for this week: Take a few minutes to find yourself a comfortable chair in a quiet place together with a relaxing drink and a notepad and pen. Reflect on what has brought you to this point, the year that is behind you and the year ahead.

Make a note of some of the events where you sense an unhelpful judgment, either from yourself or from others. Make a note of other events where you felt a sense of achievement and positive judgment.

As you review your list, realize that all of your judgments, both negative and positive, are only one point of view. Consider other angles, and think about these events from a position of love, learning and growing, as you prepare to embrace your whole self for the year ahead. With this wisdom, write down what you could do differently in the year to come.

2 Light Over Darkness

Most religions have a ritual of lighting lamps or candles to represent the light of wisdom shedding over the darkness of ignorance. If we take the essence of religion away and see this as a message for life, we can get a few profound messages:

Light only has meaning because darkness exists. Darkness is as much a part of this game as light. So, from a broader perspective, darkness is not the enemy, it's the ally that leads us to the light.

Light is wisdom. It's not being a 'good person' or doing the 'right' thing. There are countless opinions on what's 'good' and 'right', so, 'good' and 'right' do not have any universal benchmark. Light is being aware enough to understand and accept situations, and the natural consequences that flow from the choices we make. This awareness naturally shifts your awareness and turns your response into peace.

Since darkness is part of the game, we will inevitably go through periods of darkness in our human experience! By darkness, I mean we will experience various emotions like anger, sadness, fear, helpless, and other things alike. The moment we give some acceptance to that part, it no longer stays dark. Hence, if we can accept darkness as an experience of life, we will grow exponentially and see the light at the end of every challenge.

Invitation for this week: Light a candle once a day and get in touch with that aspect of your life you are judging as dark. It could be something happening directly to you or around you. Begin to see that situation through the lens of understanding and acceptance. What can you begin to understand and accept that you were previously judging? Can you also accept that part of you that was judging? Once you begin to accept, you will probably sense a change in breath and a feeling of relief in your body. You have moved through the darker feelings, and a fresh perspective becomes available to you. This fresh perspective is the light of wisdom. Embrace and accept the light as you watch the candle and feel its warmth.

3 Your Mind is the Gateway to Your Wellness

I'm happy to see that 'wellness' has become a global buzzword; most people around are finding out what to eat, where to buy their organic products, how to juice, how to incorporate a fitness regime into their lifestyle and so on. While it's great to see people make more conscious decisions about their bodies, I would also like to remind you that your mind is the gateway to your wellness.

If you are mentally stressed, anxious or depressed, the impact of your food and fitness on your health will be minimal. An easy way to think of this is that your thoughts are the primary food that you feed yourself; for your body to function optimally, it needs the utmost attention. If you have diabetes or cancer and were taught to eat rawer food because it doesn't spread the disease, but you eat it fearfully because you are afraid it may get worse. The fear is the primary thing that you are feeding your body and sadly it is likely to spread the disease!

So, while you are doing all your research on wellness to improve yourself and your family, remember to be conscious of your own mindset too as it determines how well you feel, and how you feel is the foundation for the decisions and life choices you make.

Invitation for this week: Let's start with something simple; before you eat your next healthy meal, think about the state of your mind. Are your thoughts and emotions serving you, or does this need to be worked on? If it does need work, you can start with simple meditations, affirmations or a gratitude journal to change your state.

4 Beliefs vs Desires

Many of us have long-term desires which we just can't seem to meet. Perhaps we've desired to speak confidently in public, eat healthily, become more patient, or earn more money, yet, we find that we just can't do this. When you can't get what you want, it's because there is an inner conflict going on between your conscious and subconscious mind – it's a misalignment between your desires and your beliefs.

Most of the time the conscious mind knows what it desires and has a plan on how to get it. However, the subconscious mind which holds your deep-seated beliefs is giving the opposite message. For example, the conscious mind could say, 'I need to stop eating sweets, and eat healthy foods', and the subconscious mind says, 'Sweets makes me feel safe and comfortable'. Hence, nothing changes and we continue being addicted to sweets.

Most of us don't get that the issue is far deeper than a matter of disciplining ourselves. Thus, we start judging ourselves when we don't behave in alignment to our desires, which makes us feel even worse. To help yourselves, start by having some self-compassion. Don't put yourself down for not getting a result despite all your efforts, understand that, there is something much deeper coming from your illogical mind, and those beliefs were formed right from when you were in your mother's womb.

Invitation for this week: Understand that the only reason you cannot get what you want is that you keep having a deep inner conflict between your logical and illogical minds. Affirm every night this week: "I understand that there is a part of me that may be uncomfortable in allowing what I want, and I choose to give awareness, love, and understanding to that part of me. I understand that my mind is on my side and trying to protect me in the best way possible. I love, heal and integrate all those parts of me that are holding on to past situations. I choose to believe that it's safe, right and good for me to keep moving towards what I want."

5 Leave Your Past Behind

All of us have faced some form of challenge in our past that has required us to step up, face difficult situations, and reassess our health, finances, or relationships. If you still feel plagued by events of the past, acknowledge that all those events along with the pain and drama they have caused are over now! The only way they can cause you any ongoing stress or anxiety is by reliving them, but, in doing so, you keep a piece of yourself stuck in the past going through the same trauma again and again. It sounds simple, yet so many of us have parts of our consciousness trapped in the past because we keep our judgment alive and hold on to the perspective that it shouldn't have happened.

One of the greatest gifts you can give yourself is to shift that perspective by accepting that what happened is over. Forgiving yourself and anyone else involved for not knowing any better, because you cannot change it, and focus on the lessons from the situation. Then, you can be free from the emotional pain you are carrying, while having the wisdom to move forward with a fresh perspective.

Invitation for this week: Think of one thing from the past that is still disturbing you, it could be a relationship breakdown, a situation you couldn't change, or something you did. Observe the meaning you attach to it and how you are disempowering yourself with that meaning. Finally, choose to drop your current perspective, rather, ask yourself "What lessons can I learn from this situation that can help me move forward? How can I accept what happened without judging it? How can I trust that life is working for me, and that I have the tools to handle what comes my way?" Answer that question right now, write it down, and remind yourself of that response for the rest of the week. Here's to leaving our baggage in the past where it belongs, and choosing to be peaceful over being right!

6 Away From Pain or Towards Pleasure?

What drives you to take action? Do you consciously move towards what you want, or go through the motions of the day without really being present, or only take real action when you are in crisis?

Simply put, we take action for one of two reasons: To obtain pleasure or to avoid pain. Unfortunately, most of our actions come from the latter - avoiding pain! Studies show that most actions are taken when there is crisis, and people are desperately looking to survive. Seeking pleasure comes from being inspired to move forward towards what we want, and that's where we achieve the best results. However, the more comfortable we feel, the more we take our sweet time to move forward. This is why so many of our brilliant ideas are never actualized, and all the efforts we put to take action when we are in crisis is a means of mere survival because that was all we were focusing on!

This means that we are only learning our lessons and making necessary shifts in our moments of pain and hurt. In our pursuit to avoid pain, we step up and do whatever it takes, but when have to take it to the next level, we get lazy. This is where we are at the moment, however, with awareness we can change this! Would you like to create an environment for yourself where your growth will be for pleasure and not only in moments of pain? You can use the power of your awareness to create this environment.

Invitation for this week: Think about one thing you have been too darn comfortable to start acting upon. It could be writing a book, going on a retreat, contacting someone that could help take your life to the next level. What are the costs of you not doing what is needed? Are you willing to wait until it's too late and someone else has beat you to it, or it becomes an emergency to start acting? If not, could you choose that goal over choosing anything else? Make a commitment to move towards that goal from a place of inspiration! Think about what life would be like if you achieve it. How would you feel about yourself when you know you did it? If you can imagine yourself doing it, your mind already begins to move you towards the goal. It all starts with awareness, willpower, and making a powerful decision.

7 Are You a Procrastinator?

Procrastination is no stranger to us; I have seen people beat themselves up over and over again with the guilt of being a procrastinator, so I was inspired to demystify a few things about this label:

✺ If you tend to produce great results with last-minute execution; this doesn't necessarily mean you are a procrastinator. In this case, you could have a powerful association in your subconscious mind of getting an adrenaline rush as the deadline approaches, and that's when you produce your best work and still get it done on time.

✺ If you push yourself beyond your body's capacity to achieve an overwhelming amount of tasks in a day and don't 'get it all done'; this does not mean you are a procrastinator. You just have an unrealistic expectation of what you can do, and are pushing your body beyond its capability – it would be beneficial to be kind to your body and allow yourself to rest!

✺ If you manage to complete all urgent tasks on time, but when you have non-urgent tasks, you find yourself distracted by social media. This does not mean you are a procrastinator. Again, this is more of a boredom issue and an addiction to the adrenaline.

If you are a true procrastinator, the tendency to avoid taking action would show up everywhere and all the time; in returning phone calls, in doing your daily chores, in completing assignments, etc. If you are among those who can't complete or start tasks, procrastination is a defense mechanism for you. With it, you can mentally 'escape' the things you need to do because of a deeper void. The void would most probably be something painful that you don't want to face so, it's easier to procrastinate than take any action.

Invitation for this week: Identify an area where you have been procrastinating. Check how important it really is to do that task? Is it something you are inspired to do, in which case keep it, or something that you don't believe in and you are doing it because someone told you to do it. If this is the case, you might drop it immediately.

For the tasks you are keeping, ask yourself what are you avoiding. Are you avoiding feeling like a failure, being rejected, or not feeling smart enough? Send some love to those vulnerable parts of yourself, and use the power of your will to make a decision to delegate it or do it now.

Make your decision right now, and allow yourself a moment to feel the sense of accomplishment.

8 Stop Hijacking the Past

There is great value in 'the power of now' and staying in the present, however, it's not so easy! Many of our experiences are colored by the past, and this is not necessarily a 'bad' thing if we have grown from it. Through our past experiences, we may have learned to treat our children better than the way we were treated, or learned how to communicate and stand up for ourselves. Thus, we can use the past to evolve, provided we are conscious and learn from our experiences.

However, if we are not conscious and hold onto grudges, the past can have a powerful influence on our mindset and sabotage our present. When we recall events of the past that we are incomplete with, we lose grip of the present moment and get hijacked by past trauma that we can't release. For example, we may have difficulty trusting in people because our house was burgled when we were 3 years old, and the memory still haunts us. Or we can't love our spouse fully because we had a heart break when we were a teenager, or we are frugal with money after watching our parents lose it all.

In this way, the past keeps us from living the way we want to, because we are holding onto the pain and have developed coping mechanisms to deal with those experiences. In these cases, regressing to the past is helpful for us to discover the source of our grudges, so we can finally let go of the pain we have kept inside, and collapse the coping mechanism. Regression for this purpose is therapeutic to release the toxicity from the past, so we can live in the now with awareness.

Invitation for this week: Think of one memory that still plagues you and observe how it makes you feel. It could make you feel fearful, sad, lonely, or guilty. If the memory is still potent, you will still 'feel' that toxic emotion in your body. Observe where your body has been storing this emotion as a somatic charge, place your hand on that spot and begin to gently and easily breathe out the stored negative emotions that had been suppressed in your body. Your intention of releasing that energy is enough for your mind to allow it and your body to let it go. Perform this action every day this week and notice the difference in how you feel.

9 Busting Loose From Your Defense Mechanisms

Whenever something happens that is not in alignment with what we want, we usually judge the situation as "there's something wrong", this upsets our emotions and we feel angry or sad, but over time, we find ways to cope with it and feel better.

These coping mechanisms are usually unconscious and come in the form of:

- ✺ Maintaining that we are upset with the world and becoming aggressive (the blamers)
- ✺ Pleasing others in the hope that we won't feel bad or disappointed again (the pleasers), or
- ✺ Withdrawing from the world and building a wall around ourselves to protect us from feeling hurt again (the escapers)

In all three cases, the upset hasn't left our system and these defense mechanisms slowly become a part of our identity - we become known as 'the angry one', 'the reserved one', or 'the pushover'. These strategies may distract us from our pain temporarily, however, none of these coping mechanisms truly work to make us feel better long-term, because they are born out of an upset. Instead, they become self-sabotaging patterns that keep bringing us the same upsetting situation over and over again, and end up making our defensive identity even stronger!

The only way out of this rat race is to acknowledge the original part of you that was upset and allow that part to re-interpret the initial painful situation through the lens of acceptance instead of judgment.

Invitation for this week: Take a look at the defense mechanism that you use frequently at this moment in an important relationship; are you blaming, pleasing or withdrawing? Discover the pain behind this behavior and its original source. Your original upset maybe with someone completely different like your parent, or your teacher. Allow yourself to re-interpret the original painful situation in a way that's more empowering. This subtle but powerful action can give you immediate relief and destroy your entire defense mechanism. Thus, you can be more present to life without the need to protect yourselves from your mental projections!

10 Beyond Duality

If we stop and try to remember our thoughts from the last 10 seconds, I am sure that many of us would notice examples of judgments! Perhaps, you were feeling annoyed at someone and thought they were 'wrong'. Perhaps you were reminded of something you like, or don't like.

Do you compare yourself to others, or worry about the future and judge that you can't handle what will come your way? Analyzing, comparing, and judging are a big part of our ego and are second nature to us. This keeps us in the game of needing to be 'good' and 'right' while proving that others are 'wrong' - the foundation of conflicts and wars. The result is that someone is guaranteed to feel lousy, while the others experience momentary bouts of satisfaction until they remind themselves of another situation, and the proving starts all over again!

Our need to judge and our attachment to being right has put us in a cycle of constant sabotage. So, if you feel it's time to break free from this game, why not try the opposite? Why not accept instead? Acceptance is moving beyond duality; it's your ability to be with a situation instead of calling it good or bad.

If you look at a Yin/Yang symbol of duality you can notice there is a small dot of black in the white part and vice versa; perhaps, that's to remind us that when we judge what's light, it becomes dark, and when we accept what's dark, it turns into the light!

Invitation for this week: What's one thing you are judging about yourself that you could accept right now? Understand that acceptance is not approving yourself or giving up on yourself, it's being able to be with this part of yourself. Practice 'just being' with this part of yourself for this week, without doing anything else.

If it helps, you could imagine looking at a part of you that's feeling sad for example, and just say to that part "I see you, I hear you, I have space for you, I accept that you are here, and you are a part of me." When you say it and really mean it, you will notice a feeling of ease and relief. Acknowledge the freedom and lightness that this brings you in those moments of mindfulness where you are free from criticism or resignation.

11 Goal Setting

As you move forward in your lives and continue to create goals, do you notice that certain goals appear on your list repeatedly? It could be losing weight, getting out of debt, or spending more time with family. If certain objectives keep appearing on your list year after year, chances are you will repeat the same pattern this time around too.

- Set the same target again from a place of feeling bad about yourself
- Make excuses, and occupy yourself with some other task any time action towards your goal is required
- Feel guilty and disappointed that you couldn't do it this time again despite your best efforts

Patterns keep repeating themselves until we become conscious about them and realize that doing the same things will NOT produce different results.

To succeed in achieving our goals, we need to think, feel and act differently from our previous ways. This difference can be as subtle as having a different perception of the goal or adjusting the goal itself. Since our minds are often stuck on the same track, doing even one small thing differently changes the path in your mind. Your mind needs to create new neural pathways to deal with the different thought, and suddenly, you may find that you are moving closer to what you want!

Invitation for this week: Set aside ten minutes, arm yourself with a pen and paper to review one of your important goals, and ask yourself the following questions:

Deep inside, do I want this? If you don't, it's OK! Perhaps it's something you thought you want. but don't.

What unconscious benefits am I getting from not achieving this goal? Usually, it's a feeling of not having to be "responsible" for the result.

What's more important to me, getting what I want or keeping that benefit?

How will reaching this goal make a difference in my life?

What will life look like when I achieve this goal, and how will I feel about myself?

What do I need to believe to achieve this goal? Can I imagine myself believing that goal?

What is one small step I can take now toward that goal?

Your answers to these questions would put you in a different vibrational frequency which aligns better with your goal. If you necessary, you can adjust, recreate or reaffirm your goal. Keep reading your answers to reaffirm this new perspective, work towards your small step this week, and see the shifts it brings!

12 Making Your Dreams Grow With You

Just as you grow and change as the years pass, your dreams and goals can also grow and change with you. Imagine holding on to the dreams you had when you were ten years old. At ten years, I wanted to be a cop because I thought it was cool to ride a motorbike and I wanted to save the world from the 'bad guys'!

The good news is, we can have different goals and dreams at each stage of our life, and it's okay to move through them. As we mature, we may realize that many of our goals and objectives were things we picked up from our culture, society or religion as things we 'should' do, but in fact they really aren't what we want. The impact of continuing to pursue goals that we 'should' have is a constant pressure to meet the goal, feeling guilty when we don't meet it, and feeling incongruent when we do. It's not a great place to be! Deep inside, it comes from what we learned to do as children in order to fit-in and be accepted by others. What if I said to you that you no longer need to be ruled by 'shoulds' anymore, and you are free to choose any goal or dream that YOU really want? Would you choose something different?

The more conscious you become, the more you can discover goals that are more aligned to you, and "retire" some of your earlier ones. When you let go of an old dream that's no longer relevant, it doesn't mean that you have failed at reaching it, you have just cleared space for something more authentic to who you are.

Invitation for this week: Take time to be quiet and peer deep within and identify 3 things you've told yourself you would love to achieve, because you were influenced by someone else. Imagine that you are stepping away from the energy of their influence, and give yourself the freedom to choose. You may choose the same goals, but this time it's because YOU are aligned with it. Or, you may choose to adjust parts of the goals, or to even drop those goals and choose something else. Notice how you feel when you know it's your choice, and that it will keep growing with you - you can tweak it anytime you like!

13 Confused About which Path to Choose?

With so many paths available for personal and spiritual growth, most people are confused about which route to follow. They don't know whether they need to follow Art of Living, a Guru, Hypnotherapy, Vipassana, Coaching, NLP, Buddhist chanting, or something else. My natural response to that is consciousness keeps evolving, and different things will resonate with us at different points in time, so flow with what feels right at the time without judging yourself with rules about what you 'should' do. There are as many paths available as there are people on this planet, and our ultimate role is to understand that there is no superior or correct route to enlightenment. We will all find the means to our path using the wisdom from various workshops we've done, masters we've met, and books we've read, as beautiful guides that give us gifts to add to our toolbox.

If we do this, we can see ourselves as the source of awareness who has the power to discern what tool is needed in any specific situation. Sometimes what's needed is compassion, sometimes it's understanding that we can reinterpret and reframe events of our lives, and other times it's the ability to surrender and flow. If we dissociate our identity with anyone's modality, we can align to the fact that we are humans equipped with the consciousness to differentiate between what works for us and what doesn't, thus, we can find our path to freedom. Each therapeutic modality represents a certain vibratory state, and the conveyors of their message represent our teachers, gurus or coaches. As a conscious being, we have the awareness to understand our utmost need at each point in time.

Invitation for this week: Embrace all the tools you have without judgment, and know that you are the awareness that has the power to choose what will serve you best as you evolve. Know that when you have a clear intention, and a vision of where you are aiming for, any path will take you where you want to be. From this place, choose a path that feels right for you at this moment.

Summer

A time when the seeds of spring blossom into rich abundance. A time for strengthening your valuable relationships, growing stronger and expanding into new ventures. A time for fully appreciating yourself and affirming your gifts and strengths.

14 Ready? Set? Go!

Does it feel like 24 hours is much shorter than before? It's not just you that feels that way! The Schumann Resonance which measures the Earth's natural heartbeat, shows that the Earth has been vibrating steadily at 7.83 cycles per second for decades. However, the number has been rising; in 2014 it spiked at 8.5 cycles per second and, thereafter has risen to 16.5 cycles per second. The rhythm of life does seem to be increasing.

Along with things speeding up, consciousness is also shifting to bring us more information than we've ever known. The lessons that would take many lifetimes to learn is now getting compressed into a short time, and the healing that would previously take 10 sessions is now getting accomplished in one! It has been a privilege for me to see the magic that can be done in a single session; people have been able to overcome severe phobias, decades of guilt, and long-term depression, because they are more aware and able to take responsibility for what they created.

There is now access to more wisdom than ever before, and with so much more awareness we can't pretend to be confused or helpless anymore. Deep inside you know what your biggest block is, and you also know what you need to do about it. If you think you do not know, that is your defense mechanism kicking in and doing a good job!

Invitation for this week: Think about one area of life where you feel helpless and unable to move forward. If you were to take full responsibility for all the choices you have made, identify what is really blocking you from moving forward. It's probably a belief or a fear. Now think about what you need to do to overcome that block. You have all the answers! If you step up and take action now, what could change for you? The time is now! Ready? Set? Go!

15 Take Baby Steps

If you are discouraged that you are yet to achieve your goals, I can tell you categorically that you are not alone, and it's not too late! Based on my experience, most people get stuck because:

- ❁ They lack a simple, actionable system or strategy
- ❁ They miscalculate how much time or effort is required
- ❁ They are afraid to fail or be criticized

For these reasons, people often get discouraged and quit.

Conversely, starting slowly increases your chances of completing any task. The Japanese call it kaizen which simply means "continuous change". You are taking baby steps with the big, end goal in sight.

Taking baby steps allows us to be present on the journey and gives us a sense of accomplishment when we achieve each step, both adding great value to the process. When we are present, we are using our conscious mind and intellect to move forward without getting hijacked by our subconscious patterns from the past. When we see ourselves accomplishing these small 'wins', our brain releases the chemical dopamine which in turn makes us feel good and keep going.

Invitation for this week: Think of something that you have been putting off, perhaps a change you want to make in your life, perhaps a connection that you want to make or remake with someone. What would be the first step that you could take to achieve that? How would that one, small first step represent the turning of a new page in your life? Perhaps you might even go and make that first small step now, and see what happens.

16 Stay Focused

In these days of social media, distracting apps, and demands on your time coming from every direction, it becomes a struggle to stay on track and achieve your own goals and dreams. If you want to take actions that will improve your life, it's important that you eliminate distraction as much as possible. Here are ways to stay focused in this highly distracted world:

❋ Turn off notifications

Notifications may not seem like a distraction because they rarely exceed 10 seconds, but research shows that they disrupt our thoughts for much longer and make it difficult to re-focus quickly. A proven solution is to set aside a time in the morning to work on your social media presence and check your email. Then, set aside another period to do the same in the evening or night. Stay away from your phone and turn off notifications for the remaining parts of the day.

❋ Develop a daily routine

Once you've established a routine, you can start performing your tasks in an automated fashion. You won't have to waste time to think about what to do and when to do it. Whether you are creating time for your important tasks, preparing your lunch or planning your outfit, establish a routine and more importantly, stick to it.

You can use an easy and fun app such as 'Productive - Habit Tracker' to develop your daily routine. You can download this app for iPhone: mybook.li/52ti and Android: mybook.li/52ta

❁ Multi-tasking doesn't work

Switching rapidly between tasks or doing multiple things at once completely contradicts staying focused. The solution? Fully engage with one important task. If you become bored with a task, you could designate time blocks to perform the tasks in short bursts of 20 minutes. You can designate time blocks to return phone calls, reply emails, file paperwork and run your errands.

Invitation for this week: Check your work environment and remove anything, especially your phone, that can cause you to lose focus. Allot a time to check your notifications, spend a few minutes today, not more than 30, to develop a simple, workable daily routine and stay focused on one thing at a time.

17 Identify your Most Important Tasks

If you have ever organized your day by writing a to-do list, you will know that there are some tasks on the list that are more important than the others. If there are ten tasks on your to-do list, only two of them can have a meaningful impact on your success. The other items don't matter too much in the big picture. This is the Pareto principle, in which 80% of consequences come from 20% of causes, 80% of outputs are driven by 20% of inputs and 80% of results flow from 20% of your effort.

When you apply this principle to your daily activities, you will discover that only two tasks out of the 10 tasks on your daily to-do list will be responsible for 80% of what you will accomplish for that day. When you accomplish your Most Important Task (MIT) first thing in the morning, you are already accomplished for that day, no matter what happens for the rest of the day.

Here are some ways to identify your MIT for each day. It is the task:

- ✺ You were thinking about most in the shower, the one you wrote down after your morning meditation or thought of last night before bed.
- ✺ Related to your big-picture goals whether it's a professional goal such as changing a career to move towards your dream job, or a personal goal such as finding a new apartment to move towards the lifestyle you would love.

When you are performing these vital tasks, you will hit a state called 'flow' where you are 'totally absorbed in what you are doing and you can perform them naturally, easily and impressively.'

Bear in mind that your MIT is not necessarily the most urgent. There is a clear difference between important and urgent activities. Urgent tasks require your immediate attention and if you don't deal with them, they have clear consequences. More often than not, they are associated with achieving another person's goals. On the other hand, important tasks are related to your goals. If most parts of your job involve urgent tasks, you can arrange your day such that you can accomplish your important tasks before trying to accomplish the urgent tasks, and notice the difference.

Invitation for this week: identify 3 of your most important tasks (MIT) at this moment, and create a plan in your schedule to accomplish them even amid urgent tasks.

18 A Different Type Of Prayer

Many people use prayer as a means to ask for something, and thus many prayers consist of sitting at an altar and requesting "God" or "The Universe" to make your life better by giving you more money, better health, more opportunities or a higher status in society. One way or another, we've likened prayer to a genie in a bottle, hoping that if we rub it hard enough our wish will come true. What we don't realize is that the more we desire, the more we are reinforcing lack, because desire itself comes from a feeling of not having something. The result is that we begin to operate from a feeling of void, which produces a fear of not having what we want, and then we want more.

The irony of manifestations is that you get what you want most easily when you are fine with, or without it! That's because there is more peace and less resistance when you stop focusing on the fear of not having it. So, if you are happy and content on your own and yet open to finding someone, you may attract a wonderful partner as a by-product of you 'letting go'.

Ultimately, the end-value we want through all of our desires is the feeling of peace and contentment. Hence if we use prayer as a means to connect to the vibration of "God" or "The Universe" instead of asking for something, we are short-cutting the process and tuning into the frequency of peace. The mere act of just connecting with whoever you are praying to releases you from your attachment to the desire and your peace is more permanent. This is one major reason why meditations are so powerful; it gets you to move away from judgment and desire, and connect to a state of watching and accepting the current reality.

Invitation for this week: I encourage you all to try a different form of prayer; use your prayer time as an opportunity to connect to the vibrations of the prayer you are reciting or mantra you are chanting. Connect to the frequency of the power with whom you are praying instead of asking for something. In doing so, you will realize that the state that you were asking for is right there in the connection. It's as easy and accessible as that!

19 Everything's Gonna Be OK!

In the overwhelming moments when money is scarce, your relationships are down in the dumps, you are stressed about your workload, or you feel alone… it's useful to focus on yourself and remember that EVERYTHING'S GONNA BE OK!

This takes trusting in yourself and trusting in the process of life; we've all been through challenges in the past, and it all worked out, so why will it be different now? Most of us get so caught up in our roles of being the victim, blamer or rescuer that we keep getting deeper into our drama, and the saga continues. The only way out is to have faith that life is working for you, without being attached to how or when it will happen. The higher our faith, the further we are from fear. They are opposing frequencies that cannot co-exist. Time has shown us that when we move forward just a little, what we are going through would be over. It's not the end of the world, and things will keep moving.

Look back over the story of your life, and bring to mind a time in childhood when you felt down or helpless, then move forward a little and notice that you actually got through it! When you take a good look at your life, you will realize that you have survived, you have thrived, and you are here, now! That means you know you have what it takes to work through any other low period.

Invitation for this week: Start increasing your trust in yourself and trust the bigger picture of life. Trust that you will get through all the present and future hurdles as you have done in the past. Trust that the universe has its way of maintaining an equilibrium that is beyond our desires or control, AND it's always going to be OK!

20 Is it Possible to be 100% Optimistic?

Let's be honest, do you think it's possible to be get rid of negative thoughts completely? Do you think you can avoid feeling frustrated, sad, scared, or upset? The obvious answer is No. We are emotional beings living in a world of polarity where life teaches us its lessons through various experiences. Thus, we need to view these negative feelings as a part of our life experience to fully understand the positive ones. Understand that you will experience a whole spectrum of emotions during your lifetime. You are as entitled to sadness and fear as you are to happiness and elation.

If your life's goal is 'to be happy all the time', you need a reassessment. Happiness cannot be the end goal because it represents one of the many emotional vibrations we will experience in our lifetime. Happiness is an energy that will pass through us and have an endpoint. I encourage you to consider peace to be your goal, because it represents a state of mind rather than an emotion. From a place of peace, you can witness different emotions and watch the emotional roller-coaster instead of riding in it! When you are in this place your emotions are less likely to hijack you, and you end up feeling much calmer and less upset – the natural bi-products of your state of peace.

Invitation for this week: Expect to feel down at some points in your life. It is a natural part of your life's experience, but during these 'down times,' objectively watch your emotions from a place of peace. Before you sleep review all the emotions you felt in the day again without resisting any of them. Notice the shifts you feel when you watch how you feel instead of judging them or getting caught within them.

21 What's The Worst-Case Scenario?

For most of us, the worst-case-scenario is something to dread. We do our best to avoid it and say to ourselves, 'I don't want that!' However, what we don't realize is that in doing so we are consistently thinking about it.

Anticipating and dreading the worst-case scenario is a constant trigger for stress and a foundation for anxiety. Moreover, when we anticipate the worst, we usually don't think about it long-term, and we don't trust that the bigger picture life has a way of working out everything to suit us. We are blocked by the thought of something 'bad' happening and stop right there.

Often, we get so caught up avoiding bad things that we lose out on the good things that can come from a new experience in life. Yes, we protect ourselves from a fall, but we also prevent ourselves from reaching great heights. And by worrying about the future, we are protecting ourselves from something which has never actually happened.

As some leaders such as Sir Richard Branson have done, ask yourself 'what's the downside of this situation?' Find a way to deal with it so that thought is out the way, then continue to focus on what you want. If you consciously focus on a worst-case and go through it, then, you don't have to keep living in it anymore – you can finally focus on something else and trust that all will be well!

Invitation for this week: Aim to do something totally different. Think of something that makes you anxious, then, take a moment to go through the worst-case scenario in your mind, and keep playing the movie forward until you have projected it to what life would be a year after it happened (or more if necessary). As you imagine your journey, you will discover that there will be a turning point in the pain where things have fallen into place and you feel OK!

Going through it in your mind is often more useful than avoiding the thought of the worst-case scenario, because you mind will keep drifting back to it. If you go through it, there will be a turning point where it will bring you back to equilibrium. You would realize that you cannot control things but you can have faith that things are in balance and it will always be OK. Once you've done that, you don't have to anticipate the worst-case anymore because you've come out the other end realizing it wasn't so bad.

22 The Happiness Formula

Happiness, just like any other emotion, is a transient experience of life. This means that it's not a permanent state of being; all emotions have a beginning, middle and end, which is why we call them "energy-in-motion". However, because most people think it's possible to cling to emotions, we have to put some effort in to keeping that energy flowing. Happiness has become that one emotion that people crave for most, thinking it's possible to "always be happy".

I have found that a valuable way to look at happiness is to allow it when it comes and experience it to its fullest, knowing that it is a moving energy that will transform to something else. Peace is a state of mind that we can have permanent access to, happiness is something we can welcome and watch as it comes and goes. Perhaps happiness will transform into peace, or perhaps into action, or even into a sense of achievement.

To have more experiences of happiness in our lives, we can break it down to a formula to see what we need to do in order to increase the frequency of this emotion.

Our body releases four types of happiness hormones:

- ✺ Endorphins: These are produced when you are doing what you enjoy, exercising and having a hearty laugh.
- ✺ Dopamine: This is produced when you feel a sense of accomplishment and achievement.
- ✺ Serotonin: This is produced from a sense of contribution and giving back to the world, and also from being in natural light and the open air.
- ✺ Oxytocin: This is generated from feeling a sense of connection in your relationship with other beings and also from doing something you love with friends and family.

Hence to have more happiness in your lives, you simply need to keep your body moving with exercise, cultivate close relationships where you feel a sense of love and connection, learn things to keep your mind growing and accomplishing, and do something to contribute back to our planet.

Invitation for this week: As you move around this week, pay attention to your energy. Even if you're only walking in your local area or around your office, you're moving. Notice even your smallest achievements and items you've crossed off your 'to do' list. Notice the sun on your skin as you walk outdoors. Finally, notice how it feels to spend time, connected with people who are special to you, even if you're not doing anything in particular. Notice how all of this feels for you, and realize that this feeling is happiness.

23 Perfect Imperfections

No one is or will ever be 'perfect' for long; both in your own eyes and in the eyes of others. You may experience moments of what you consider to be perfect when what you get is in alignment with you expect. Then, you will soon realize that something changes, and that state doesn't last for very long. There are many people that strive for perfection, and end up living life oscillating between anxiety when they are anticipating a result, and disappointed when the result doesn't match their expectation.

Wanting perfection is a tough standard to meet; especially when you realize that there is no road map and no one knows how to meet this standard, because you have created it and your interpretations keep changing! If you look at what you love most, perhaps your pet, or your favorite flower, or your children, you will notice that they are far from flawless, and yet there is something that draws you to them. They are here to show us the beauty in the way nature has created them, and you love them from it. If things were always impeccable, we wouldn't have anything to learn, shift or grow from. We tend to focus inwards only when there is something uncomfortable on the outside, and we grow when we can eventually accept what we have judged. Hence, the reason why the universe has created things to be in perfect imperfection, is so we can learn a deep lesson of acceptance and seeing beauty in the way things are. Nature has created you in the same way too, and there is immense beauty in the way you are, only if you look for it. For a moment assume that there is no such thing as imperfection, and there is absolute perfection in you and everything around you, how do you feel?

Invitation for this week: Look for the perfect imperfections that surround you when you give up the need to be perfect. Take 5 minutes now to write down the magnificence you notice in your surroundings right now. Then during the week notice what you have been judging about yourself and trying to control so that you can be perfect, and free yourself from that job. Try on accepting the imperfections in you and around you, and notice how you feel

24 Intention is Everything

Take a moment to focus on your communication in intimate relationships. Conflicts in intimate relationships are bound to happen. My key message to all partners, parent-child, siblings and close friends is: Intention is Everything!

Conflicts arise when we feel something is unjust, someone has wronged us, or they have not met our expectations. When in conflict, we often take the role of the victim or the prosecutor... And we are in the drama! In those moments, we feel like the person has wronged us, and we don't look at their intention. The simplest way to get out of the drama is to trust that in loving relationships, there is no intention to hurt. The misalignment is either coming from both parties focusing on their pain rather than thinking of the other, or doing what they think is best for the other without checking-in. Blaming doesn't help because the other person feels attacked and by default, starts to defend, which creates 'war'.

Acknowledging that the other person's intention is positive is a great start to resolution and creates listening from both parties. From a place of being heard, both of you could say where you are coming from and have an intention to find a resolution that will not cause pain to either party in the future.

Invitation for this week: Identify any conflict you would like to resolve with a loved one. Think about what the intention of the other could have been, understand that it was not to hurt you and pull yourself out of the drama.

When you feel a sense of release, have a conversation with the other person from a place of understanding. Without blaming them, share how you felt and what hurt you phrasing it like "I felt hurt", instead of "you made me feel hurt".

Share what you have learned from this situation, and discuss solutions on how you can translate your positive intentions for the other person in a way that works for them, and how they can do the same for you.

25 Failure vs Rejection

Relationships are the catalyst for much of our learning and growth! When there is relationship conflict, we get triggered. We put on our defenses and suppress how we are feeling. The truth is these feelings don't stay buried forever, so suppressing them doesn't make us free. The feelings wait below the surface until we are triggered again and can explode when we least expect it.

I have found that the core feeling we suppress in relationships is either feeling rejected or feeling like a failure. I would say 50% of people have a rejected trigger and 50% have a failure trigger, and the irony is that these two groups of people can often get together and trigger each other! The one with the rejected trigger usually wants a lot of reassurance, time and acknowledgment from their partner to overcompensate for inherently feeling not accepted. And the one with the failure trigger takes up more projects than they can handle, prioritizes work, and keeps thinking about how they can be more successful to overcompensate the inherent feeling of failing.

So, you have one person becoming more and more needy for affection, and the other one becoming more distant and needing space. The result, as you can imagine, is slowly hell breaks loose in the relationship because no one's needs are met! Of course, big healing will be to address the root of the trigger, however, this is an individual issue that often stems from childhood and not something that your partner can do. What we can do for our partners at best is to avoid triggering them!

Invitation for this week: Think about your primary relationships and understand that your partner might have the opposite needs, values, and triggers to you. Spend some time to understand if you and your partner are more impacted by failure or rejection, and make a conscious effort this week to give your partner what they need – either more reassurance or more space. A by-product is that you will probably get more of what you need too!

26 Do You Control Your Destiny?

The question of whether we are bound by destiny or we have a free choice has been debated for a long time. Some people believe that we create our lives day by day, others believe that everything is destined and we are just going through the motions.

One way of looking at this which has resonated with many of my clients is that life is similar to playing a game of chess with a computer. You choose to play the game and you determine your moves, but regardless of the moves you make, the consequential moves of the computer are already determined. If we extrapolate this concept to life, existence itself is a choice we made at a different level of consciousness, and because of that choice, certain things are consequential that we call destiny.

The destined consequences of our lives are what show up on our birth charts and astrology reports, as 'fixed events', things that we have to go through no matter what happens. We are responsible for it all, and we cannot even blame the 'fixed events' because they are the consequences of the choices we have made at some level. Hence, the only way to be free from the dilemma of destiny or free choice is to be 100% responsible for the life you have created and be fully responsive to it. Thus, you are free from being the victim of life since what happens at each moment of your life are the consequences of your past actions.

Invitation for this week: Choose to wake up every morning feeling fully responsible for the life you are living, not blaming yourself, but taking ownership from a place of peace. Say to yourself that "I choose to take complete ownership for the life that I am living, I accept that all that's occurring and all that has occurred is the consequences of the choices I've made in the past". Then, use the power of your intention to visualize what you would like to create from this place and the choices you can now make. Do this for one area of life at a time for you to gain better clarity and achieve tangible results.

Autumn

A time to reap the rewards of your hard work, to enjoy abundance, to build up your reserves, to prepare to slow down, to enjoy the fruits of the time and energy you have invested in yourself.

27 Manifestation 101

As you step into a new phase of your life you may start to think about what you would like to create and accomplish – this is a great way to start because without a vision, we cannot create. Everything starts with a thought, however, turning that thought into reality takes clarity, belief, action, and trust. Please give yourself 10 minutes of quiet time to do this.

Here are some simple yet powerful steps to manifestation:

- Know where you are now
- Determine where you want to be
- Discover how you are going to get there
- Let go of the attachment

Do a mental check of your current situation in life. If you rate your happiness from 0-10 with 10 being the highest, what would your score be? What aspects make you unhappy?

Where is it you would love to be? Make it specific and measurable so you are completely sure you have reached that space. Create a goal that is attainable within the next 3 to 6 months so you set yourself up for success. otherwise, our mind may see afar off and decide to give up. If your goal is long- term think of what you can achieve in the short-term that is part of the long-term.

What steps can you take towards your goal? Create a list of simple, actionable steps, making it highly specific and suitable for you to imagine. Your subconscious mind works better with images so the more specific the better. Define dates, days, times to make it very clear.

Let go of your attachment. When you get clarity about what you want and start taking action towards it, learn to be OK when you don't get it. If we are OK with or without our goals, our vibration changes completely from lack, which is what happens when we want something, to trust, and from this space, there is no resistance and so manifestation is so much quicker!

Invitation for this week: Follow the steps above to uncover what you want. Then, visualize yourself getting it, feel all the positive emotions related to it in your body. In your mind, step out of that picture, freeze it and imagine that you are covering it in a ball of light. Allow yourself to feel that you are whole and complete with or without that goal. Surrender that ball of light to the universe and mentally let go of its form, but retain the positive feelings in your body. For best results, do this visualization every night before you sleep

You've identified what you want, and let go of the attachment to the result... now just watch!

28 More Than a Single Thought Creates Our Reality

Most people interested in personal development are seeing the power of their thoughts in creating their reality. If you think about it, can a single one-off thought create the reality you desire? It's less likely because there isn't enough potency of energy in that for it to manifest instantly. For example, if you think that you will receive a billion dollars and this thought occurs once, it's probably not going to define your destiny. The reason that thoughts have so much influence in our lives is that we tend to repeat the same thoughts over and over again, then, turn them into beliefs. Hence, it's the repeated compression of the same thought vibration that creates our reality.

Research shows that we generate between 60,000 and 80,000 thoughts per day, 98% of these thoughts are our beliefs which are the same as yesterday, and 80% of these thoughts are negative! If all it took was repetition to create these beliefs, all it needs is repetition to come out of it and create other beliefs that can serve us better!

This is how mindfulness and meditation works, it puts us in a different vibratory state with focus on peaceful thoughts for some time, which makes us feel more uplifted.

Again, meditating once will probably be insufficient to shift your entire reality, its repetition will gradually give you a different experience of life. With awareness, we can consciously break the patterns of the past by creating different practices and rituals.

Invitation for this week: Take a moment to review your day and notice a time when your mind-chatter is at its peak. It might be during moments where you are not in action, like the 3 pm boredom point in the middle of work, or just before bed. Then, commit to a new 5-minute ritual to change the conversation in your head by meditating, repeating a powerful affirmation, reading an empowering book, or listening to an insightful discourse. In 7 days, you will start seeing shifts in your state of mind, and within 3 months, you can have shifted your reality.

29 Letting Go of a Fear of Failure

Take a moment to consider the following questions:

✷ Personally, how do you define failure?

✷ When was the last time you failed?

✷ What lessons did you learn?

For some people, failure is an opportunity to start afresh with a renewed energy. For others, it can be demoralizing. For all of us, failure is important feedback that supports our growth.

We learn our fear of failure through our early experiences at home and at school. Just imagine - without the judgments of others, how would you even know that you had failed? Remember some of the everyday activities that you are happy to repeat until you achieve success, without judgment.

Let go of your fear of failure by:

✷ Failing fast. To improve anything, we need to let go of what came before, and the faster we do that, the faster we learn and the faster we can improve.

✷ Recognizing judgments. Failure and success are two sides of the same coin. Do you remember where you learned to judge your results?

✷ Focusing on action. An easy way to guarantee that you'll never fail is by avoiding action. This might seem like a safe option, yet it's also the easiest way to lose sight of your dreams.

- ❈ Accept how you gain from failure. It's easy to focus on the negatives of failure, yet it also has its advantages. Take a moment to reflect on how it has benefited you in the past, even indirectly or with the benefit of hindsight.
- ❈ Focusing on the present. You are here, now, as a result of all of your actions in the past, and those actions included your failures, your successes and everything in between. All of this made you who you are today, so celebrate your present as you look to a future of learning and discovery.

Invitation for this week: Notice all of your tiny failures as you go through your daily routines. Notice the times that you forget your keys, that you take the wrong route, that your shoelace comes untied, that you put off a task that you said you would finish.

When you've done that, notice the tiny everyday failures and mistakes of the people around you. Notice how most of these just don't seem to matter at all. Notice how easily people self-correct. Notice how easily you self-correct, when no-one is judging you and you are free to learn.

From this, discover what failing really means to you and notice how easily you can let it go when you focus on how far you have already moved forwards.

30 Changing your Standards

You only have to look around the average city street to see posters, billboards and magazine covers that portray an idealized version of 'perfection' that is hard to live up to. Even though we know that those images are computer-enhanced, they still work their way into our unconscious thoughts, serving as reference points for the idea of perfection, or at least, what we think other people might expect perfection to look like. Retailers know only too well how these unrealistic comparison make us act.

Perfection is not an end state but a process of perfecting, of improving something in comparison to a role model or benchmark. If we go through life unaware of those comparisons, we are destined to seek out anything that holds the promise of making us perfect. A perfectionist, then, is not someone who lives life to the highest standard. In fact, the truth is the opposite. A perfectionist is someone who is afraid that they never quite measure up.

If you recognize yourself in the following examples, you might be a perfectionist.

- ✤ Are you always waiting for the 'right time' to act, to live your dreams?
- ✤ Do you tend to repeat your mistakes instead of admitting to them and learning from them?
- ✤ Do you focus on flaws and shortcomings instead of gifts and achievements?

Often, a perfectionist is striving to achieve an unrealistic or unattainable standard - not because that standard is too high, but because they don't even know what the standard is, since it has been set by someone else. By realizing this, and taking control of the standard, the perfectionist can master their wonderful ability to strive for excellence and create standards which are attainable and even rewarding. Instead of pushing yourself to always achieve more, notice the areas of your life that might become neglected. Allow your high standards to support your journey and be a role model for others, through love, understanding and learning.

Invitation for this week: Notice when you find yourself repeating a task, or pursuing a task after you have completed it, for example coming back to a work project after it should have been completed, or spending more time in the gym than you promised yourself, or going back to the wardrobe to choose another outfit for a meeting. Ask yourself what it was that made your first attempt 'not quite good enough' and ask yourself, 'good enough *for whom?*' Is it you? Or someone else. Finally, ask yourself what is really important in this, and what your objective is. Set yourself a standard, achieve it and move on to your next achievement.

31 Letting Go of Controlling

We all need to feel in control of events in our lives - it's how we form our basic sense of security, and when we feel secure, we feel free to be ourselves and explore our dreams. On the other hand, if someone or something causes you to lose that feeling, you might lose confidence and become reluctant to take risks and try new things. You realize that security is not something that anyone else can give you, and yet, still, sometimes that need makes you want to control situations around you. Of course, that can also lead to friction, when other people are trying to control the same situation at the same time!

If you sometimes feel that your need to control is causing conflict in your life then here are some ideas that you can try out.

- ✺ The need to control is strongest when we feel out of control, so step back and think about what might be happening in your life which makes you feel less secure than normal. Address that issue directly, rather than trying to control other things as a substitute.

- ✺ Take a moment to consider your objective or desired outcome. For example, if you're trying to control which TV channel you watch or where to go for dinner with a friend, think about your objective. Is it the activity, or is it spending time with someone important? Once you realize your destination, the route can become much less important.

- Invest time in planning the things that are most important in your life, and control the aspects which you can realistically control. If it's not part of your plan then it's unlikely to interfere in your personal goals and needs. Let someone else take care of it.

Invitation for this week: Make time to notice the things that you can control, and make them as good as you possibly can. For example, you can control how you brush your hair, or how you make your coffee, so do it to the best of your ability. Then, notice the things that you don't control yet don't usually think about. The time the sun sets, for example, or the weather, or the movement of the waves on the ocean. Notice how it can even feel good to let go of certain things in life. Finally, notice the things that you can easily entrust to others, giving you more time to focus on living your life as only you can.

32 Is There a Logical Reason for Illogical Behavior?

Most of us have had some emotional outburst or behaved irrationally at some point in our lives. What I'm talking about is having an emotional reaction that's out of your control and possibly, out of your character. However, when you think about it in retrospect, it doesn't make any logical sense why you did that, which leaves you even more frustrated.

The first thing to understand here is that your irrational behavior isn't coming from your logical mind, thus, trying to rationalize it won't help! These outbursts are highly emotional and come from a part of your mind that has been carrying all the toxicity you suppressed over time when you didn't process your feelings. These feelings are usually the uncomfortable things we want to avoid, like guilt, failure, rejection, incapable, etc. All these things we've pushed down have now accumulated, and eventually, a small thing that reminds us of the same feeling can trigger this barrage of suppressed emotions, and result in an over-reaction or an outburst!

Invitation for this week: Please don't try to use your logical left brain to rationalize the behavior or the emotional right brain – they speak two different languages! Instead, connect with the emotion behind the outburst, were you feeling scared, angry, helpless, or guilty? Allow yourself to feel it despite the discomfort, and understand that there's a deep part of you that has been feeling this way for a long time. Acknowledge those emotions and begin to take some deep breaths to process it until you finally release it.

33 Being an Adult

We are trained for many things through our upbringing, however few of us were taught what we are truly responsible for. Our understanding of responsibility usually comes from judgments we have created by observing our parents and environment. As a result, when we grow older, we operate from one of two positions:

1. As a 'Parent' to everyone, feeling overly responsible for other people's well-being, trying to fix things for others, and doing beyond what's necessary.

2. As a 'Child' where we are not responsible for anything and rely on someone else to take care of us, fix our problems, and clean up our messes.

Interestingly these two personalities tend to find each other and often end up getting married or becoming best friends where one is constantly rescuing the other; after all they need each other to keep their role alive! Consider the distinction that operating as an 'Adult' means that you are fully responsible for all the choices you have ever made and the consequences of them, nothing more! You do this by taking accountability for all your choices, actions, interpretations and feelings, without judging yourself. Instead you are aware of your behavior, and are willing to learn from it if it doesn't work.

Invitation for this week: Think about where in your life have you taken on being accountable for other people's actions, or avoided being accountable for your own actions? What would be different if you took complete responsibility for your own part?

34 Healing Your Inner Child

One of the biggest things that influences us is unhealed traumas of our past. You may have heard of the term "inner-child" before and I want to shed light on it.

An inner-child is a younger part of yourself that is stuck in the trauma of the past. By 'younger', I mean younger than today. It doesn't have to be a child below the age of 18. If something happened to you yesterday and you didn't deal with it, then the suppressed upset emotions stay in your body and remain stuck in the moment of the trauma. This becomes your inner-child.

One of the most useful things we could do for ourselves is to keep healing those parts of us that are stuck in the past. What you need is a release of your toxic emotions, then, feel loved and accepted. A great way to give love and acceptance is by having an inner dialogue with your younger self, and feed them with the love they have been craving.

Invitation for this week: Create bookends of the day where every morning before you get out of bed, and every night before you sleep, you tell yourself:

I am loved

I am accepted

I am safe

I am worthy

I am enough

I am special

I am important

The more you say this to yourself, the more it raises your self-esteem and you slowly recover from the situations of the past. If you have young children, these are great affirmations to tell them before they sleep to strengthen their self-worth.

35 How to Love You?

Have you ever noticed that we tend to love others in a way that feels good and convenient for us? Some of us may like to show love by cooking and create amazing culinary experiences – but we forget to check if our loved ones are hungry or feel like eating! Some of us may offer coaching or advice when our loved ones just want to vent or aren't ready to hear it. Some of us may buy beautiful presents as a way of showing love, when perhaps what was needed most from us was our time!

This isn't about blame - this is usually a subconscious response that we are not aware of. However, if we look at this consciously, we can see that we tend to love people in a way that makes us feel good for loving them without checking whether or not, it makes them feel good!

Being aware of this concept can be a game-changer because if we intend to give love, we can finally be aware of what would make the other person feel loved and do it that way.

Have you ever thought of what makes your partner, child or best friend feel loved and appreciated? It could be direct actions like hugging or saying "I Love You", or indirect such as giving them space. You may find that what they want is different from what you have been doing! If you don't know, ask them, and this could be the start of an interesting conversation, creating intimacy and understanding.

Invitation for this week: I invite you to pick one person in your life, discover what truly makes them feel loved, and begin to love them in that way. The law of reciprocity says that once you start giving in this way, you will also begin to receive love in a way that makes you feel loved too, from the same person or someone else!

36 Loving Yourself takes More than a Massage

By now most people understand that loving themselves is not selfish, it's necessary! Yet many people think that the way to love themselves is to buy a nice bag, have a fancy dinner, or get a massage. To determine whether or not, this is an expression of loving yourself, consider the intention behind your action? Are you doing it because everyone else does it, and you want to be a part of it? Are you trying to please someone else or the society? Or are you doing it because you have determined what makes you happy and this is what you are inspired to do at this moment?

When it boils down to it, are you in touch with what you want? Or does it feel like your desires have come from opinions you've picked up along the way? It's never too late to start discovering who you are and give yourself what you want, even if it doesn't agree with what you've been told in the past. Perhaps what you've wanted was just time to yourself, or time to dance and be free.

When we are very young, we are in touch with what makes us happy. However, as we become adults, we begin to pick up influences from our environment and feel like we need to adhere to those influences before we can be accepted.

As a result, our self-validation becomes associated with what we think others want from us, and we begin to lose touch with what we truly desire.

Loving yourself is getting out of this 'pre-conditioning' and getting back in touch with what we truly want or need.

Invitation for this week: I invite you to look within, and ask yourself whether you need the approval or acceptance of anyone else at this moment. Ask yourself, what would I love to do? What would make me happy? Then create a plan to do it in the name of self-love!

37 Selfish, Selfless, or Self-Love?

Typically, we have three common feelings when we do things for ourselves; some of us feel righteous and lose the sense of anyone else, some feel a sense of guilt because we believe it's 'wrong' to cater to our own needs, and some feel a sense of peace. We oscillate between a state of being selfish, selfless or at peace. Our natural response to this comes from our beliefs, conditioning, and experiences.

Here is a typical journey of response: Many of us were taught that to be a good person, we need to sacrifice and put others before ourselves. Thus, we constantly give away our time, energy or resources, and we perpetually feel guilty every time we even think solely about ourselves! Then, after years of feeling short-changed or being used and discarded, we may decide from a place of pain to 'stop giving'! The result is that we swing to the other end of the pendulum where we only think of ourselves, feel righteous about it and just stop caring about anyone else. Unfortunately, this still doesn't give us inner-peace and we can sometimes end up losing meaningful relationships!

So how do we find the balance? Let's break it down; first, we need to understand the difference between selfish love, selfless love and self-love. Selfish love is thinking of yourself and nobody else. Selfless love is thinking of everyone else and not yourself. Self-love is right in between; considering what would be loving for yourself, and being loving to others at the same time. Self-love comes from a place of inner peace where you understand your responsibility to love yourself first, then your responsibility to be loving to the world.

For example, if you wish to set a boundary, move away from saying "yes, I will do it" and feel miserable, or saying "No! Go F*#% yourself!" and feeling angry. Instead set conscious boundaries that honor all parties, such as "I understand this is important for you, it doesn't work for me because xxx, so let's think of a better way we could address this together?" When we come from this space, there is self-love present, we have consideration for others, and we are at peace.

Invitation for this week: Think of where you are being overly selfless or overly selfish. What would be the self-loving response to this situation? Make a decision to release your guilt or anger right now, then, come from a place that is loving to you and the other parties involved. Ensure that you communicate total self-love during the week.

38 Self-Love on Special Occasions

As children, most of us have thoroughly enjoyed our birthdays and special occasions because we had no expectations around it. We would be present at the moment and bask in the glory of whatever showed up. As we got older, we began to judge and create conditions such as "only if I received flowers, that means he loves me", or "only if I am wished at midnight, then I am special", or even better "the price of the gift shows how much I am loved". All of these lead to expectations that cannot be met all the time. Consequently, these special occasions have become associated with disappointment, and end up reminding us that we don't have what we want.

The underlying issue, as is often the case, is our interpretations and expectations that aim to prove that we are in charge. What if on the next special occasion, you give up wanting a certain type of behavior from another person, and focus on displaying loving behavior towards yourself and strengthening your relationship with yourself?

Invitation for this week: Think of the next special occasion coming up - valentine's day, birthday, new year, or anniversary, then, drop all your "shoulds" around it! If you are single, drop any notions of "I should be in a relationship". If you are in a relationship, drop any notions of "s/he should behave like this". For your next special occasion, forget your need to rely on other people to make you feel special, and if they do, it's a bonus! Set some time to think of one loving act you will do for yourself on this occasion, and be present for whatever else shows up during the day!

39 Transitions

Most of us have gone through transitions in our lives, leaving school, getting a job, getting married, getting divorced, bearing children, having career shifts or moving from one country to another. The fact that your transitions are taking place means at a deeper level there is consent from you, the universe and the people involved. From a metaphysical perspective, something cannot take place unless there are consent and logic at a higher level of consciousness. You may not, and perhaps will not understand it at the moment, and therefore all you can do is manage your state of mind. You could resist it or embrace it.

The best way to approach transitions is to have faith in ourselves and in life that we will handle it, like we have handled all the rest that has happened for us. Transitions are pre-destined to create shifts. Through dealing with the changes in the outer environment, we learn to grow, adapt and develop new ways of being that keep taking us to the next level of consciousness.

What is required in these moments of transitions is trust; trust in ourselves and trust in the bigger picture that things are occurring in the way they are meant to occur.

Invitation for this week: Think of one change you are resisting to embrace. What could you learn from it if you embrace it? Where are you holding onto fear? If you had faith that this transition is for your best, what could be possible?

Winter

A time for reflection, for slowing down, for looking back, for cleansing and for preparing for renewal. A time for building acceptance and resilience. A time to take stock, to relax, to pause, to learn, to recover.

40 The Magic 30 Minutes of Your Day

Did you know that approximately 30 minutes before you sleep, you are most naturally susceptible to receive messages that go directly to your subconscious mind? This is when your conscious mind begins to lose control and move further to the background, your defenses are less, your brainwaves are moving to the theta state, and you become highly impressionable to anything you think, read or hear.

Your subconscious mind gets updated every night with the events of the day during your sleep, and it starts with the very last thought you had. Many of us tend to listen to the news, think of our daily stresses, or catch-up with the latest gossip on social media before going to bed. The message we are receiving from all these sources can be disempowering and gets stored straight into the deepest recesses of our minds.

Hence, if we sleep feeling anxious, we will wake up feeling stressed. In this sense, how you feel in these magic 30 minutes is highly important, because the night dictates how we feel in the morning. So why not use this this time to reinforce loving messages to yourself, or use this time to visualize what you want? If you were to understand that whatever you think or feel before sleeping can become a hypnotic suggestion, what kind of messages would you like to input into your mind? My suggestion is to do a daily review, breath out any stresses or emotions that are still bothering you from the day, then, declare positive affirmations to yourself before you go to sleep.

Invitation for this week: Think about your state of mind before going to bed, does it serve you? Use your magic 30 minutes to review your day and release the thoughts and emotions that are still impacting you. Then, take 2 minutes to repeat a positive affirmation, or mentally list ten things you are grateful for before going to bed. I invite you to try this, and in just three days, you will see the difference it makes to you when you wake up!

41 It's OK!

This week I ask you to be with a simple but powerful message "It's OK!" fundamentally, you are saying 'OK' to who you are, and how you feel. Many people feel that they need to be on the fast-track lane to become enlightened. Thus, they start looking at everything from a 'higher' perspective and it's not OK for them to feel anything other than happiness, love or peace.

The truth is that most of us are not enlightened yet, we continuously feel other emotions than happiness and peace all the time. There are three major 'negative' emotions that we feel right from birth and will continue to feel throughout life, these are fear, anger, and sadness, these three emotions are also called primary emotions. Both animals and babies feel these emotions because they are innate emotions. They are not the result of any societal rules or judgment. When we are threatened, we are scared. When our boundary is invaded, we are angry, and when we feel a sense of loss, we are sad. All other emotions such as guilt, betrayal, embarrassment, are secondary and come after we have judged something as not being 'right'.

So why not say OK to how you feel and allow yourself to go through it, instead of placing more rules on how you 'should' be? In our lives, we will feel angry, sad and fearful. The gifts from these emotions is that anger helps us draw boundaries, fear helps to protect us, and sadness helps us to release and cleanse our system. If we don't allow ourselves to experience these primary feelings, we will experience the secondary emotions which are even more uncomfortable like remorse, shame, frustration and humiliation and all the rest that come from judgment.

The only way to overcome this feeling is to allow yourself to feel it and go through the experience consciously. You have to acknowledge the discomfort, say yes to your emotions with the intent of bringing yourself back to your default state of peace. This allows you to experience the natural ups and downs of life with more ease and flow.

Invitation for this week: Simply scan yourself for how you feel right now, then say OK to yourself for it because it is your truth. Repeat this action every morning and you can set the tone for the day to say 'OK' to yourself.

42 What Gets You Triggered?

I bet you have been triggered many, many times. What I'm talking about is when something evokes an emotion in you, and you lose your sense of balance. It could be because you were not invited to a party which made you feel rejected, or you made a simple mistake and felt like a failure, or someone made a joke about your appearance and you felt inadequate. Triggers can occur at any time and have the capacity to completely destabilize us, by opening up old wounds of the past.

When you are in charge, you feel in control and present to what is going on. However, when you are triggered, you can suddenly be overtaken by an old feeling that you tried to suppress in the past without realizing it. For instance, if you suddenly find out that "everyone" has been invited to an event, except you, it can remind you of being at school and not being picked for the sports team which made you feel so rejected that you concluded that "I don't belong". In your present day the old feeling of "I don't' belong' still comes up and you react to something that doesn't matter to you!

The only reason this can impact you so much is that the beliefs and conclusions of the past are deeply embedded in our subconscious mind, which is far more powerful than our logical mind. The good news is that it is possible to heal this and overcome these triggers provided you know them.

Invitation for this week: Practice being mindful to the present moment, and remind yourself that you are the adult of this moment, not the child of the past. The easiest way to snap out of your trigger is to shift your state to being PRESENT to the moment. The more you are present, the less you are in the grip of the hijack. Simple ways of being present are to be mindful of the now, practice mindfulness meditation, and focus on what's happening around you NOW.

43 When is it OK to Scream, Swear and Punch?

We know that screaming, swearing and punching are socially unacceptable, and we accept that this is not appropriate to be done to another person. However sometimes when these things are done privately as an act of release, it can feel so good! The truth is that we all feel angry at some point, and if this energy of anger is not expressed outwards it implodes inwards and starts affecting our bodies as tension and disease.

The act of intentionally expressing suppressed emotions and releasing toxicity in a safe environment is known as catharsis. If the suppressed emotion is anger, it's probably not going to express itself by sweet-talking, but by roaring out that rage. Catharsis is a pivotal point of any therapy because it is the final release of all the energy and emotions that are trapped in the mind and body. It's only after this release that we are finally able to see clearly and get a different perspective on an issue.

By this, I am not encouraging you to lash out at somebody, rather am asking you to find a safe space to allow yourself express your pent-up emotions in their authentic form and be done with them for good!

Invitation for this week: Give yourself permission to find a safe space, focus on something you are truly angry with and let it out fully. If need be you could punch a cushion, swear, scream, sing, dance, shake it out and do whatever you need to do without holding back! Just go to town with it and make it a ritual for yourself that nobody needs to know about!

44 Acceptance is All You Need to Be Free

At the core of it, all our relationship traumas are caused by judgment; we judge others, they judge us, and we both judge ourselves! The opposite of this judgment is acceptance, which is why it is the basis of healing. Our instinct to deal with behaviors we don't like is to either reject it or tolerate it. These two methods keep us stuck in the same vibrational realm of judgment. Thus, our relationships become inauthentic, and our pain gets deeper.

Let's look at all these approaches more closely.

Rejection: Rejecting a person because of what they did doesn't stop you from being upset about it, you can cut-off with someone and remain angry at them for years.

Tolerance: Even if tolerance is a virtue, it still has its limits because it makes us feel resigned and cynical instead of being at peace since underneath it all we are still judging. In other words, tolerance makes life bearable, it doesn't make life joyful. This approach can also cause feelings of depression or even numbness.

Acceptance: Let's not confuse acceptance with approval. I am not saying that you need to approve people that lie or cheat. What I am saying is to accept the fact that that they did what they did, and it's over! This is merely stepping up a notch and accepting fact without any interpretation or judgment. Just see it as something that happened without attaching any meaning to it. For instance, "she stole money from me" is a fact, you are taking away the "how could she, how dare she, she's such a cow, she is so immoral…". By doing this, you instantly collapse your plethora of toxic emotions and feel lighter. Once you accept what a person did, your response is up to you; you have the choice to understand and maintain that relationship as it is, end the relationship, or place a boundary in the relationship. There is no right response, and whatever resonates with you after acceptance will be the right response, because it will be from a place of peace.

Invitation for this week: Think of a relationship that you are upset about and check whether you are tolerating the person or rejecting them. This could also be a relationship with yourself. Look at your upset, separate the fact of what happened from your interpretation, and accept that it happened! From that place, see what would give you the utmost peace in this relationship – continuing it, ending it or placing a boundary?

45 Surrender – the Only Way to Go

Have you noticed that there are times when no matter how bad you want something, how hard you pray for it, and how many times you visualize getting what you desire, it just doesn't go your way?! I'm sure you know what I'm talking about, and although it feels difficult, these are the most 'teachable moments' that life presents to us. This is where we learn that our conscious inputs cannot guarantee that someone will love us or our situation will change, the only way out is to let go.

When we feel like we have done everything but the situation is the same, we have two options; to get angry at life and God for being so unfair to us, or to look again at the situation with acceptance and get out of the drama! One of the fundamental truths we are living with is that we will experience duality, there will be both light and darkness in our lives, there will be experiences that are both pleasant and unpleasant. The only thing we can fully control is our interpretation of the situation and our responses.

Praying for a result doesn't always work, as our conscious mind cannot control what is meant to be, and often doesn't see the big picture or know what is right for us in the long-run. Praying for strength to handle what comes our way and to 'accept things the way they are' is far more empowering and something we can fully control. Accepting and surrendering to the current realities changes our filter from 'why me? This is so wrong!' to 'I have what it takes to handle this situation'. It gives us the power to be with people and situations without judging them, gets us out of the role of being a victim who is suffering, and keeps us far more centered and grounded. You get to a place where you are OK with or without the situation changing, which is extremely freeing. If things do shift, it's a bonus, but if not, you are still OK.

Invitation for this week: Think of a situation that has not changed no matter what you have done, and understand that the only thing you can change about it is your filter. Go down the route of surrender and acceptance by taking some time to acknowledge that you have the strength to handle this situation and know that you are OK with or without a change to this situation.

46 The Play of Opposites

We discover life by understanding duality. This means that you have a better understanding of life by understanding opposites – the ability to compare and accept difference. Unfortunately, most of us reject 50% of duality by judging the dark parts as 'wrong' or 'bad' instead of classifying them as a natural experience of life. Thus, we reject parts of our darkness and the darkness around us.

What if instead of pushing away feelings of anger, sadness, and fear, we recognize this as a regular part of our life and begin to accept this in ourselves and others? For starters, we would be much more at peace, and the so-called darker feelings would pass much quicker because there will be no resistance. Happiness and sadness are transient experiences. All emotions are 'energy in motion', something we feel in our mind and body for a short time until it passes. Happiness, sadness, excitement, and anger are all short-term experiences. Lightness and darkness are equally important, and our job is to allow both into our world without judgment.

I know this is a tall order and it's not so easy – but that's part of the game of life! Instead of trying so darn hard to be light and positive all the time, why not accept the times we naturally feel different. In this case, you can aim to be in a constant state of 'peace', which is far more attainable rather than a constant state of 'happiness'!

Invitation for this week: Look at your light and dark parts through the lens of acceptance. Understand that you will experience a spectrum of different emotions. Thus, it helps to develop an inner acceptance for all of it. It doesn't mean that you need to act on your darker emotions or indulge them. Saying that it's good to feel them is also judgment, your best option is to accept that they are there and allow them to pass.

47 Clearing Clutter with Emotional Attachment

Does your home seem to get a little smaller every day? Do you find yourself holding onto mementos and souvenirs? Perhaps your wardrobe seems to get smaller every time you try to find the right outfit?

We're all attached to objects - symbols of who we are and what is important to us. These objects might be gifts you've received, or photos, or art works, or souvenirs you've bought to remind you of special places. Collecting such symbols is completely normal, but the reality is that you only have so much living space. At the same time, it can be unthinkable to consider throwing anything out.

Some people regard physical clutter as a sign of mental and emotional clutter. They say that holding onto objects is a way of holding onto feelings and relationships. Maybe that's true, and perhaps that depends on the amount of space you have!

Whatever the reason, sometimes you might find yourself holding onto things longer than you need to, both emotionally and physically, and you might benefit from gently letting go.

Consider your relationship with the objects you've collected like any other relationship. Some good aspects, some not-so-good, and always something that has enabled you to learn and grow. Therefore, the key to de-cluttering is not being 'tough' with yourself, it's the opposite. To clear space in your home and your heart, gratitude is the key. When an object has served its purpose in your life you can thank it, enjoy some fond memories, be grateful to it and allow it to move forward in its own journey. Whether it's an item of clothing or an ornament, it has given you something, and now it could be time for someone else to enjoy it. It's not just a thing, it's a symbol of something important in your life. If it wasn't somehow important, it wouldn't be taking up space in your home!

Make space for the things that are important, that communicate who you are right now, and who you choose to be in the future.

Invitation for this week: Look around your home. Consider that everything around you was placed there, by you or someone else, with purpose and intention. Ask yourself if that object still serves its purpose, or if it is time to say 'thank you'.

If it does, take time to enjoy that purpose. If not, allow it to move on to a new home.

If you feel that the time has come to say thank you then perhaps you have already made the decision to let go.

48 From Pain to Peace

A word of warning, if you've discovered how to live consciously through reading, attending workshops, or meditating, it doesn't necessarily translate into actually living consciously. Conscious living is a choice we make every moment, especially in the painful moments. Part of being conscious is being able to accept that pain is one of the things we will face in our lives on earth, but as many of us know, suffering is a choice. Suffering comes from us interpreting our pain as being bad, wrong, and something that shouldn't happen to us.

What if we chose to reinterpret the experience of pain as a part of our life plan? First off, it may actually reduce the periods of pain because when we accept consciously it instead of judging or being resigned to situations, they don't have the same hold over us. Secondly, we can choose the channel the pain as fuel to learn and grow from. All exponential growth is the byproduct of overcoming periods of pain and turning things around. If you took a moment to play any breakthrough experience in slow motion, you will see that the growth is in those moments where you made a powerful choice to think differently and stop being the victim of circumstances. It could be to finally decide I don't deserve to be abused anymore and end a relationship, or choose to stop punishing ourselves for mistakes we've made in the past.

Invitation for this week: I invite you to think about what pain have you been facing recently, and what would be a new way to interpret this without making yourself the victim? I encourage you to apply these questions to the current situation that's been happening and find a way to grow from reinterpreting all that's happening around us.

49 Leading By Example

Leading by example is one of the foundations of good parenting. Children learn how to behave from how we treat them and others, by watching us and getting used to what is 'normal'. As a child, you might remember some of your influences, and how you felt when you discovered that other families had different definitions of 'normal'. Maybe you had some friends whose home life you thought was strange, and others who you secretly envied?

As an adult, what you expect from others has been influenced by your own childhood experiences, and you pass those expectations on to other people; not only your own children, but other people too who you influence, perhaps as a manager, teacher, friend or some other role model.

Learning to respect others begins with self-respect, and self-respect begins with understanding and accepting yourself. When you are able to accept yourself fully, you can accept those around you. You might find that there's a certain person who knows how to 'push your buttons' and that person is reflecting back an aspect of yourself that you may not have fully accepted yet.

As a child grows and learns from its parents, it also reflects back its parents behaviors, mannerisms, language and personality. Such a mirror can be difficult for a parent to accept, and it can be easy for parents to fall into the trap of expecting their child to behave in the 'right' way, despite the example set by the parent.

Your relationship with your child is very much a reflection of your relationship with yourself, and your own inner child. The pain that is unhealed in you can easily be passed onto another generation, and you also have the power to choose a different path.

As a child grows and matures, they develop more of their own personality and preferences, and yet you will always see yourself reflected in them. Begin by choosing what you want to see in them, and accept that, as a parent, you can choose how you behave as a role model.

One day, your child will become their own role model, and as you look forward to this day, you can see how your love and acceptance heals the past and creates a better future.

Invitation for this week: If you have children of your own, consider how they serve as a reflection of you and think about how you can appreciate fully their honest, accepting love for you. If you don't yet have your own children, you might consider how your everyday actions build the world of the future, and how you influence the children in your family and social network through your interactions with others. Leading by example is about doing what feels right to you, even when no-one is watching.

50 You Have a Choice

When healing any aspect of our lives, giving acceptance to those parts of us that we have judged in the past is so important. Our issues arise from judgments we have made about ourselves, other people, results, or situations. Judging something as 'good' is no better - when we judge something positively we are reinforcing that something else will need to be 'bad' or 'wrong' in contrast.

Peace comes from accepting all of yourself, and understanding that your whole self has enabled you and supported you this far in life.

A simple way to be free from any worry or challenge is to recognize that we have a choice in how we interpret things. We can choose to keep judging events and people and live life by being pulled between feelings of rejection and joy. We can also choose to understand that life offers us a wonderful choice of experiences that can be both easy and challenging, and our job is to examine them through the same lens of acceptance.

It's OK to get caught up by events in the moment, it's OK to forget yourself at times and react to what's happening around you. What is most important is that you take time to reflect, learn and accept. You might not feel that you have a choice in the moment itself, yet you can create choice for yourself for next time. What matters most is your intention.

Invitation for this week: Choose one thing that's challenging for you this week, such as a relationship or a task at home or work, and begin to notice all the things you are judging about it, including other people's behavior, your behavior or the situation. Imagine that you can step back and accept these things as they are without feeling the need to change them. If you encounter an obstacle on your path, you find a way around it. As you do this, you can observe that the more you accept, the lighter you feel as you yourself from the constraints of judgment.

51 Pause to Reflect on the Year

If you look at this past year through the lens of "what can I learn from my experiences this year", you would probably find more learning and growing opportunities than ever before! We all know that staying in our comfort zone doesn't really inspire growth; when things are fine we tend to repeat the same behavior, and live a pretty robotic life without much awareness. Instead when there is chaos, we wake up and find our inner resources and deal with it, and then we grow.

This past year has given us many opportunities to learn patience, acceptance, resilience, and a deeper level of trust that life will be OK despite what things look like. We have also seen some motivational coaches and leaders be publicly questioned for their integrity, again this is an opportunity for us to see the humanity in these beings and learn that there is no hierarchy in the human tribe.

The more we compare, separate people into 'us' and 'them', and put some people on a pedestal higher than others, the more we are buying into judgment and creating divide. This year has provided plenty of opportunities for us to either buy into this game, or make a new choice to be free of judgment, accept what has happened and look inwards to learn.

What has this year taught you?

Invitation for this week: Take a moment right now to hit the pause button and reflect.

Pause to reflect on the changes, challenges, accomplishments, and setbacks that have happened in the last week.

Pause to listen to yourself. Do a mental and emotional check-in of how you are feeling right now.

Pause to see if you have picked up the lessons from the past, and whether or not you are working towards implement those lessons?

Pause to think about what you would like to improve in your life, and assess what you would need to do to bring it to life.

Pause to process all that has happened this year, find peace, and start the next year with clarity.

Acknowledge yourself for all that you have achieved this year. Aim to start another year with more love, acceptance, and peace.

52 A New Beginning

As we reach the end of this book, the next part of our journey begins. Together, we have explored the thoughts for conscious living that can bring you greater awareness, greater happiness and greater action to achieve your life's dreams.

Being here, now, is a valuable idea to acknowledge. You have grown through all of life's challenges. Like a forest, you pause for the winter and then begin afresh in the spring, ready for whatever new surprises life brings to you.

When you're looking for new inspiration, you can return to the section of this book that speaks to your needs, and offers you guidance in finding your own answers. Then, you can take time out to consider the invitation, and create your own conscious thoughts – for action.

Your happiness is your responsibility and your right, and it is within your power. You have everything that you need, and you can be everything that you want.

Begin now. Take the insights you have already discovered and begin living consciously in every moment as you create it.

I hope that we will meet again and share our conscious thoughts as we continue this wonderful journey together.

Invitation for this week: Begin the cycle again. Look through the book from the beginning and take a moment to notice how far you have already grown, how much you have left behind and moved beyond and how much you have accepted into your life for the better.

About Sonia

Sonia Samtani is the founder of All About You, a leading mental wellness centre in Hong Kong offering counselling and therapy, training, transformational workshops, and personalised products to support you in your own healing process and life journey.

Sonia is a coach, practitioner and hypnotherapy instructor, and has led workshops and courses since 2005. Her practitioner-training courses have seen hundreds of graduates pass through her centre, inspiring them to transform their lives and support others with their healing and evolution. She has also developed her own signature workshops, healing modalities and techniques, which have been adopted by her graduates and wellness colleagues globally.

Sonia has successfully addressed a multitude of issues for clients and students, including resolving phobias, overcoming anxiety, healing depression, shifting limiting beliefs, releasing trauma, finding one's life purpose, releasing physical pain, and overcoming loss.

Sonia is a sought-after mental health expert and public speaker. She has been featured on TedX and in the media including the South China Morning Post, Vogue, Cosmopolitan, Marie Claire and Tatler.

Sonia's passion is to raise consciousness, which is reflected in her bespoke services. She founded All About You to inspire you to realize that your life really is "all about you"; your thoughts, interpretations, and beliefs which have contributed to creating your current reality. Life mastery simply requires you to become aware of what you have created and accept all that you have previously judged.

Sonia's vision is to empower individuals with simple, yet powerful tools to navigate through the ups and downs of life with awareness and acceptance, so that they can tune into the magnificence of who they are.

Her invitation to readers is to set the intention that every day they can be more aware and accepting than they were yesterday.

You can discover more about Sonia at her website:

soniasamtani.com

Workshops and private sessions can be booked via the All About You centre:

www.allaboutyoucentre.com

Praise for Sonia's Work

"Sonia is an experienced therapist, coach and teacher. Her keen sense of perception accurately helps identify root causes. She patiently helped me discover and define the genesis of the blockages I wanted to overcome. She is trustworthy and non judgmental and her methods empowered me to see my greater picture."

Menka Amin

"Since Sonia became a part of my life, I discovered my most valuable privilege; an education to experience more truths than those given to me since birth and to use those truths to master my own mind and be liberated from irrational beliefs and other forms of self-coercion. Her guidance has led me to live a richer and fuller life and I am deeply grateful for this continuous education of life itself."

Claudia Got

"I have worked with Sonia for over two years. Her standout gift is how she thoroughly tailors her extraordinary knowledge and intuition to my needs."

Dr Enzio von Pfeil

"Often times when you are in search of improving your life, you tend to overlook the obvious, which is in front of you or just outside of your field of vision. When the universe put Sonia in my life, not only did she help me open my eyes through hypnotherapy, but has empowered me with the tools to keep my mind open, marriage happy, playfulness with my kids, and most importantly, grow within. Thank you Sonia!"

Lance Chiu

"Sonia is a gifted therapist, teacher and speaker. She has evidenced her passion for what she does through all trainings and workshops I have attended with her over the last 2+ years. She has the ability to make abstract and difficult concepts make sense and has been an integral part of my personal transformation and development."

Angela Hancock

"The sessions that I have had with Sonia have been life changing. As a result of working with her I am now my most authentic self. I have let go of old beliefs about my life and myself that kept me from living an abundant life. I now feel more empowered and accepting of who I am."

Stormie Sandhu

"I was out there, and all over the place; desperately looking for a solution in hopes to help myself. Until I stumbled across Sonia's hypnosis service. Then I began to change. Moving away from being a victim, to a person looking for wisdom.

It's as though you enter a portal, where you are guided by this beautiful lady, and then you learn to stop judging yourself; and begin to find your potential, life force, healing, sensuality, wisdom, love and compassion... thank you Sonia."

Grace Lee

"Things really connected in a deep level when I attended your Inner Child workshop. It gave me a glimpse of my inner world that I had not seen before. That started showed me how my outer world is being created by my inner world. Upon attending Level 1 of Hypnotherapy Class, my God, suddenly the clarity and interconnection of me, my Life and my World started to make sense. Since then, it has been a ride of discovery of how I had been creating my reality / life situations and healing where needed. Thank you so much for showing me a new world and possibility in my life."

Jessica Syvones

"Sonia Samtani - the woman that has impacted my life enormously. Sonia is very inspirational, professional, motivational, changing & shifting mindsets to discover the better version of yourself. She has an emphatic heart and very precise leadership - I couldn't express enough positives about this wonderful, independent, strong businesswoman, that Sonia is. All About You Centre - is my second home and Sonia is a friend for a lifetime. She leads by example and will always make you accept yourself. My biggest lesson from Sonia: "if you forgive someone it means you still think this person has done something wrong but if you accept - this brings you to a completely different level.." and she has let me discover the meaning of acceptance. Thank you, my Dear. I can only highly recommend the services of Sonia, the one I have done until now are: Fast Tracking, Hypnosis, Tarot reading, NLP practitioner coach training course, Public Speaking etc I'm still looking forward to the Inner Child Healing and the NLP master course. Sonia, you have changed my life - I will be always grateful for this. It takes a village to raise a child but it takes only Sonia Samtani to impact and shift to become the better versions of ourselves."

Patrycja Slawinska

www.ingramcontent.com/pod-product-compliance
Lightning Source LLC
LaVergne TN
LVHW041259080426
835510LV00009B/796